How
Devo

With Scones, Strawberry Jam
and Clotted Cream

Geoff Wells

Authentic English Recipes
Book 7

Cover Artwork & Design by
Old Geezer Designs

Published in the United States by
Authentic English Recipes
an imprint of
DataIsland Software LLC,
Hollywood, Florida

https://ebooks.geezerguides.com

ISBN-13: 978-1976179815

ISBN-10: 1976179815

Table of Contents

DEDICATION

This series of books are dedicated to Mildred Ellen Wells 1906 - 2008

Mom lived for 102 incredible years. She went from horse drawn carriages and sailing ships to bullet trains and moon rockets.

She was not a fancy cook but everything she made tasted great. My dad grew much of what we ate in our garden so everything was always fresh and free of chemicals.

This book is a collection of some of her best recipes. I have just translated the quantities for the North American market.

I know she would be delighted to see all her recipes collected together so that you can continue to make these great tasting dishes.

Geoff Wells - Ontario, Canada - September 2012

Introduction

Devon is one of my favorite areas in England. If I was to go back to live I would most likely choose Devon.

It is the South of England and enjoys the best climate with warm summer days and gentle sea breezes.

The coast is dotted with quaint fishing villages that have changed little in hundreds of years.

After a day of sightseeing by the time 4pm rolls around you'll probably be ready for a spot of tea. So it's good that the tea shops are so easy to find. Just squeeze yourself into one of the little tables and order a Devonshire Tea.

Devonshire tea is not a tea blend like Earl Grey or Orange Pekoe, it is a ritual performed everyday in small tea rooms throughout Southern England and particularly the County of Devon. A favorite pastime for both locals and tourists this tradition should definitely be on your to-do list whenever you visit Devon.

Real English tea with milk, fresh hot scones with homemade strawberry jam and mounds of clotted cream are what is on the menu at 4 o'clock in the afternoon.

This is an occasional indulgence so don't stress over the calories - just enjoy it.

How to Make Real English Tea

Order tea in any North American restaurant and the odds are good that you will get a pot of warm water and a tea bag on the side. This will make flavored water but it will not make tea.

There is probably nothing you can do about restaurant tea - besides avoiding it - but at least at home you can get it right.

Real Tea

Tea is an infusion made from leaves, loose tea is just chopped up leaves. The loose tea leaves go into the tea pot and when you pour the tea you use a tea strainer to catch the leaves before they get into the cup.

Tea Bags

There is nothing really wrong with the idea of tea bags. The problem is with the big food corporations that are always looking for ways to save a buck. Consequently the quality of the tea in the bags tends to be less than that of loose tea. Along with tea leaves you will often find tea dust.

Tea Balls

The compromise is to buy a tea ball that allows you to put loose tea in a small metal ball that has holes in it. This gives you the convenience of a tea bag and the quality of loose tea.

Of course you will still have the problem of finding loose tea in North America. Even in Canada it is not available in most supermarkets and your only option is to buy it from a specialty shop or online.

Making a Cuppa

Even if you are stuck with tea bags, you can do a much better job than any restaurant. An American restaurant is the worst place to get a decent cup of tea.

Boiling Water

Unlike coffee, which should never be boiled, tea requires boiling water to release the full flavor.

Warm the Pot

If you pour boiling water into a cold teapot much of the heat in the water will go towards warming the pot. To prevent this, either warm your teapot with hot tap water or use a little of the almost-boiling water from your kettle. Just pour some in the pot, swirl it around a bit and pour it out.

Add the Tea

Add your loose tea or tea bags to the warm pot. How much tea you use is, of course, a matter of personal taste depending on how strong you like it. Our rule was always one teaspoon per person plus one for the pot. But, like they say, "your mileage may vary".

If you are using tea bags, then one bag per person is probably a good place to start. But you can usually get enough for two cups from one tea bag if you use a pot.

Bring the Teapot to the Kettle

Water will stop boiling as soon as the heat source is removed. So, if you take the kettle from the stove to the pot, the water will not be boiling when you pour it on the tea. So the rule is - always take the pot to the kettle. When the water is at a rolling boil, pour it into the pot as quickly as you can.

Steep It

You need to allow the tea to sit and steep for 5 minutes to allow the flavors to get from the leaves and into the water.

Traditionally, at this point, you would cover the teapot with a tea cozy which was sort of a quilt made to fit the pot with openings for the spout and handle.

Milk, Sugar or Lemon

You can have your tea black or add various combinations of milk, sugar, honey or lemon. Don't put milk and lemon together as the lemon will curdle the milk. Another nice touch is to serve warm milk rather than milk from the fridge since the ice cold milk will cool the tea.

Recap

Warm the teapot using hot tap water or almost-boiling water from the kettle.

Swirl the hot water in the teapot and then pour it out.

Place the tea (loose, in a tea ball or tea bags) in the warmed pot.

Bring the teapot to the kettle and when the water is at a full rolling boil, pour it into the teapot as quickly as possible.

Steep for 5 minutes. If you have a tea cozy, put it on while the tea is steeping.

Enjoy your tea black or with whatever additions you like.

How To Make Scones

Ingredients

> 2 cups (240g) white all-purpose flour
> 3 teaspoons (15 mL) baking powder
> ½ teaspoon (2.5 mL) salt
> 2 tablespoons (25g) sugar
> ⅓ cup (65g) shortening
> 2 large eggs, slightly beaten
> ½ cup (120 mL) (approx.) whole milk or cream

Method

Pre-heat the oven to 425˚F (220°C, Gas Mark 7).

In a large bowl, combine the flour, baking powder, salt and sugar. Mix well.

Cut in the shortening with a pastry blender until the mixture resembles a coarse corn meal.

In a separate measuring cup add enough milk to the slightly beaten eggs to make ¾ cup (175 mL). Mix well.

While stirring with a fork, add just enough of the liquid mixture to the flour mixture to make a soft dough.

Continue to stir until all of the flour disappears.

On a lightly floured surface, knead the dough for about 30 seconds

Either pat the dough down, or roll it out, to about ½ inch (1.25 cm) thick.

Cut into rounds with a cookie cutter. You should get 10 to 12 scones.

You can re-use any scraps left over from cutting the dough by reforming and cutting again.

Note: Only do this once. After that the dough will become too tough and too dry.

Place the scones on a greased baking sheet.

Bake at 425°F (220°C, Gas Mark 7) for 12 to 15 minutes.

Serve warm

How To Make Strawberry Jam

Ingredients

2 pounds (900g) fresh strawberries, washed, dried, hulled and lightly chopped
4 cups (800g) white sugar
Juice of one lemon

Method

Put the strawberries, sugar and lemon juice in a large saucepan.

Over low heat, cook until all the sugar dissolves.

Turn up the heat to medium-high an bring to a full, rolling boil.

Boil rapidly, stirring frequently, for 15-20 minutes. The jam should be fairly thick.

Remove any froth from the top and remove saucepan from heat.

Pour into warm, sterile jam jars and allow to cool before sealing.

If jam is going to be used right away, refrigerate it after it has cooled. It will keep for about 2 weeks in the fridge.

If you want to keep it for longer, store in the freezer and thaw when needed.

Sterilize Jars

The easiest way to sterilize jam jars is to place them in your oven and bring the temperature up to 350˚F (175°C, Gas Mark 4). Don't go any hotter as you may crack the glass. Put some newspaper on the shelf and lay the jars down so they don't touch each other.

Heat them for 20 minutes and use a good quality oven mitt to handle them.

Fill them while hot with the hot jam mixture.

You can also run your dishwasher on a rinse cycle timed to finish when your jam is ready. Only use this method if you have a sanitize setting on your dishwasher.

How To Make Clotted Cream

Clotted cream is a process. You start with unpasteurized cream and by slowly heating it, clots will form on the surface. It is easy to do but does take a long time. Is it worth it - absolutely.

Ingredients

4 cups (950 mL) unpasteurized whipping cream

The problem of course is that you cannot go to the grocery store and buy unpasteurized cream. So you have to make do with pasteurized cream. Avoid the ultra-pasteurized cream because it won't work.

Just buy whipping cream with the highest fat content you can find, probably 40%.

If you have happen to live in a dairy area and can persuade a local farmer to sell you unpasteurized cream then you are in for a real treat.

Method

Find an oven safe pot with a lid and pour in the cream. It should be a couple of inches deep but a little more or less is not critical.

Put the covered pot in the oven for 8 to 12 hours at 180°F (82°C)

The cream will form a think yellowish skin - that's the clotted cream.

Let the pot cool to room temperature then put it in the fridge for another 8 hours.

Scoop the cream off the top and put it in a serving dish. What's left in the pot is still good cream and can be used for baking.

SERVING

Traditionally the tea should be served with milk but if that's not the way you like it, don't do it. Homemade strawberry jam is always served with Devonshire Tea but if you have to buy it at least use a good quality preserve that has whole berries.

You can even buy scones at the bakers but there really isn't a substitute for the clotted cream. Don't let anyone tell you whipped cream is just as good because it's not the same at all.

Air Fryer & Instant Pot Methods

I guess when it comes to these new fangled gadgets, we're a little late to the party, but they have now found an important place in my and Vicky's kitchen.

We use these new appliances so much we decided to re-release the Authentic English Recipes series with Air Fryer and Instant Pot directions for all appropriate recipes.

We have also added videos for all these recipes to our

https://instantpotvideorecipes.com

membership site.

As one of our loyal readers you get a free membership to this site as a bonus for buying this book. All you do is visit the secret claim page to get your 100% discount coupon code.

https://fun.geezerguides.com/freemembership

Instant Pot Strawberry Jam

Making strawberry jam in your Instant Pot is a little easier than making it the traditional way. It requires less stirring and is less messy because it eliminates those inevitable splatters that occur when using a stovetop method.

Ingredients

2 pounds (900g) strawberries, cleaned, stemmed and roughly chopped
2½ cups (500g) granulated sugar
4 tablespoons (60 mL) lemon juice, preferably fresh

Method

Place all the ingredients in the Instant Pot and select the Sauté mode. Mix well and continue stirring until all the sugar has melted.

Turn off Sauté mode and place the lid on the Instant Pot. Turn the valve to "Sealing".

Select Manual mode and set for 6 minutes. When time is up, use a Natural Pressure Release.

Once the pressure is released, remove the lid and stir the jam.

If you want a less chunky jam, mash the strawberries using a potato masher. (optional)

Select the Sauté mode and allow the strawberries to cook for approximately 10 minutes. It should start to feel thicker.

Carefully spoon the jam into sterilized Mason jars while still warm and seal the jars "finger tight". Allow to cool on a wooden cutting board. The metal lids should seal as the jam cools. If any do not seal properly, use them first.

The jam should keep in the refrigerator for 2 to 3 months or in the freezer for 6 months.

Instant Pot Clotted Cream

Clotted cream is a must with Devonshire Tea but can be rather fiddly and time-consuming to make.

This Instant Pot recipe makes it much easier to achieve amazing results so that you can, indeed, have an authentic Devonshire Tea experience.

Ingredients

4 cups (950 mL) heavy cream (whipping cream) Note: DO NOT purchase ultra-pasteurized cream as it won't work.

Method

Pour the cream into Instant Pot insert and close lid and set the value to "Sealing".

Set Instant Pot mode to Yogurt Boil. To achieve this, press the Yogurt button and then the Adjust until you see the word "Boil".

When Instant Pot beeps, indicating that the boil setting is done, press the Keep Warm button. The Keep Warm mode maintains the temperature between 145°F and 172°F (63°C to 78°C).

Leave on the Keep Warm setting for 8 hours.

Turn off Instant Pot, remove the lid and remove insert. Place the insert on a wire rack to cool. Be careful not to agitate the cream too much. Agitating will cause the cream to mix back into the milk liquids underneath, reducing the amount of clotted cream you end up with.

Allow the cream to cool for about an hour at room temperature.

Cover the pot with plastic wrap and put in fridge for at least 8 hours, again, being careful not to agitate the cream.

After 8 to 12 hours the clotted cream will have thickened.

Using a slotted spoon, gently skim the thick layer of clotted cream from the surface, leaving the whey behind, and ladle into a jar or bowl. Sterilized Mason jars would work well.

This recipe will yield about 2 cups (480 mL), perhaps a little more, of clotted cream.

If you like your clotted cream to be a little less thick, stir some of the whey back into it.

DON'T throw the whey out! You can use it to make Whey Scones.

Refrigerate the clotted cream and use within 4-5 days.

Also refrigerate the whey and use it up within 4-5 days as well. You can substitute whey for buttermilk in any recipe that calls for buttermilk.

Whey Scones

After you've made your clotted cream, you won't want to waste the whey. This recipe makes lovely, fluffy scones and uses the leftover whey.

However, if you don't have any whey, you can always substitute buttermilk or regular whole milk.

Ingredients

> 2 cups (240g) all-purpose unbleached white flour
> 4 teaspoons (20 mL) baking powder
> 2 tablespoons (30g) cold butter
> 1 cup (250 mL) Whey

Method

Pre-heat the oven to 425˚F (220°C, Gas Mark 7).

In a large bowl, combine the flour and baking powder. Mix well.

Using a pastry blender, or two knives, cut in the cold butter until the mixture resembles breadcrumbs or a coarse oatmeal.

Add the whey, mixing just enough to combine.

Turn the mixture out onto a lightly floured surface and gently knead to form a smooth dough.

With the palms of your hands, press the dough out to a thickness of about ½ inch (1.25 cm) overall.

Use a 2 to 2½ inch (5 to 6.3 cm) round cookie cutter to cut the scones out of the dough.

You can re-use any scraps left over from cutting the dough by reforming and cutting again. Note: Only do this once. After that the dough will become too tough and too dry.

Gently place the scones, close together but not touching, on a lightly greased baking sheet.

Brush each scone with a little whey (or milk).

Bake at 425˚F (220°C, Gas Mark 7) for 12 to 15 minutes or until golden brown.

Remove from the oven and allow to cool on a wire rack.

BONUS ~ Claim Your Free Book

Thank you for buying this book! As a bonus we would like to give you another one absolutely free - No Strings Attached

You can choose any of the books in our catalog as your bonus. Just use this link or scan the QR code below -

https://fun.geezerguides.com/freebook

Please Review

As independent publishers, we rely on reviews and word-of-mouth recommendations to get the word out about our books.

If you've enjoyed this book, please consider leaving a review at the website you purchased it from

If You're Not Satisfied

We aspire to the highest standards with all our books. If, for some reason, you're not satisfied, please let us know and we will try to make it right. You can always return the book for a full refund but we hope you will reserve that as a last option.

About The Author

Geoff Wells was born in a small town outside London, England just after the 2nd World War. He left home at sixteen and emigrated to Canada, settling in the Toronto area of Southern Ontario. He had many jobs and interests early in life from real estate sales to helicopter pilot to restaurant owner. When the personal computer era began he finally settled down and became a computer programmer until he took early retirement. Now, as an author, he has written several popular series including: Authentic English Recipes, Reluctant Vegetarians and Terra Novian Reports, to name a few. He and his wife (and oft times co-author), Vicky, have been married since 1988 and divide their time between Ontario, Canada and the island of Eleuthera in The Bahamas.

Find all of Geoff's books at

https://ebooks.geezerguides.com

Follow Geoff on social media

 https://facebook.com/AuthorGeoffWells/

 geoffwells@ebooks.geezerguides.com

About Our Cookbooks

Quality

We are passionate about producing quality cookbooks. You'll never find "cut and pasted" recipes in any of our books.

Consistency

We endeavor to create consistent methods for both ingredients and instructions. In most of our recipes, the ingredients will be listed in the order in which they are used. We also try to make sure that the instructions make sense, are clear and are arranged in a logical order.

Only Quality Ingredients

To ensure that all of our recipes turn out exactly right, we call for only fresh, quality ingredients. You'll never find "ingredients" such as cake mixes, artificial sweeteners, artificial egg replacements, or any pre-packaged items. Ingredients, to us, are items in their natural (or as close to natural as possible), singular form: eggs, milk, cream, flour, salt, sugar, butter, coconut oil, vanilla extract, etc.

English Speaking Authors

We write all our books ourselves and never outsource them or scrape content from the Internet.

Published by Geezer Guides

When you see *Published by Geezer Guides* on any book, you can be confident that you are purchasing a quality product.

About Geezer Guides

Geezer Guides is a small independent publisher that only publishes original manuscripts. We will never sell you something that has just been copied from the Internet. All our books are properly formatted with a clickable table of contents.

Other Books You May Like

You can find our complete catalog at

https://ebooks.geezerguides.com

Plus Many More

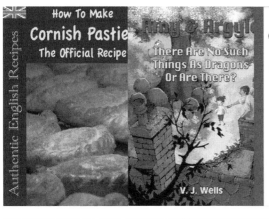

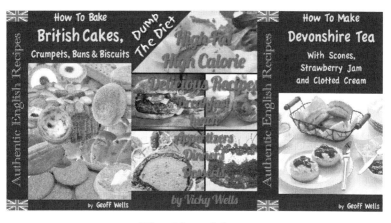

Plus Many More

Printed in Great Britain
by Amazon